Echoes Carved In Moonlight

Poems Woven from my Dreams and
Memories

Isabella Ullas

BookLeaf
Publishing

India | USA | UK

Made with ❤ on the BookLeaf Publishing Platform
www.bookleafpub.in
www.bookleafpub.com

Dedication

To my guiding stars, the hearts that lift me:
my mom and brother

Preface

*From the very start, I realized that writing is not just
something you do, it's a voice, a pulse, a way to reach out
to hearts beyond my own. This book is the collection of
thoughts and emotions I have poured into paper, not for
fame or recognition, but for the simple hope that
someone, somewhere, might feel a little less alone, a little
more understood.*

*Every poem, every passage, every fleeting thought here
comes from the deepest corners of my heart. Some
tender, some raw, some messy, but all are real. I wrote
them because I needed to, because I had to speak the
things that lived quietly inside me.*

*If even one word resonates with you, if even one line
whispers something you've been feeling too, my heart is
fulfilled.This is not just my voice,it is an invitation to
connect, to feel, and to remember that our hearts are
never as separate as they sometimes seem.*

*So, I offer these words to you, imperfect and honest,
hoping that they find a home in your heart as they have
found in mine.*
-Isabella

Acknowledgements

To my mother, Dr. Elizabeth John, thank you for nurturing my dreams, for your endless patience, and for always believing in me even when I doubted myself. Your love is the foundation that allows me to pursue my passions fearlessly.
You are my role model and my pillar of support.

To my brother, Paul Ullas thank you for being my companion, my critic, and my cheerleader. Your presence in my life adds both joy and strength, and I am forever grateful for your support and love.

This book is for you, for helping me find my voice and encouraging me to share it with the world.

1. Nostalgic soul

Those who cherish memories are my kind of people.
The world says look ahead but I love to cherish the
memories as well as the future.
Some memories clear as the water,
and some faded as a whisper.
Memories that are close to our hearts,
a treasure to hold onto.
The feeling of nostalgia when you hear
your favourite song you used to love
and know by heart.
A lot of memories hidden,
like a song in the heart.
I vibe with nostalgic souls.
The ones who have hearts that remember,
and the ones who live in memories.

2. Fleeting time

Slipping through our fingers,
that we don't even notice how time goes.
Time is like a river,
it keeps flowing whether you notice it or not.
Time slips by so quickly,
that the stickers saved for special occasions,
and the sparkly treasures you once cherished remain
untouched.
The clothes you adored soon grew too tight,
as time flows on like a river.
Time is like a book full of secrets,
everyday is a page and you don't know how many
chapters are left.
The moments we cherish turn into memories.
One day, we'll cry remembering the times we laughed,
and laugh remembering the times we cried.
As time flees by

3. The Art of Healing

The slow mending of a broken heart,
broken pieces that are never meant to be apart.
Longs to be whole again,
yet kept apart by pain.
Like an artist's play area,
my heart became messy, emotions took shapes.
Mistakes turned into discoveries,
and my heart into an art like kintsugi.
Piece by piece becoming whole again,
Clinging tight through loss and gain.

4. Strangers again

We went from best friends to strangers;
isn't it weird how time changes us.
I used to know everything about you, but now I pass by
you, pretending I don't know you.
Its sad but it happened,
and all I can do is think about it.
Our friendship began as we sat together in class, slowly
learning about each other.
And now we are strangers with memories together.

5. The myth of perfection

Perfection is just an illusion,
Nobody's perfect
and everything doesn't have to be perfect.
Like art, poetry, nature and life
everything beautiful is not perfect.
It's okay if your friendship isn't perfect,
flaws and quirks makes friendship real.
It's okay if you stumble over your words,
it just makes you a human.
Sunset doesn't need perfection to be a ethereal,
as no two clouds are the same.
Even Broken Glass can paint rainbows.
So embrace your flaws,
as a messy garden can still bloom with radiance.

6. Through the seasons

Seasos change,
Feelings change,
Closer than ever,
Yet as far as possible.
Loving and hoping,
for something to happen.
Like a lover's quarrel between the rain and wind,
or the slow dancing of the sun kissed flowers.
Snow flakes and raindrops waiting to be spilled,
while the quiet town sleeps through the seasons.

7. A thousand tiny hugs

Hugs, the most beautiful form of communication,
they talk without words.
Making a person feel loved and know they matter.
Its so underrated that,
sometimes you only need a hug to feel better.
An undying power of a hug,
that words combined cannot match.
Hugs like magic,
healing the broken.

8. Echoes of myself

The girl who loved dancing non stop and jumping on beds.
The girl who would kick and scream when tickled.
The girl who becomes so excited that she would plan her outfits in advance.
The quiet, kind and sweet girl,
who kept all her worries bottled up.
The girl who was there for everyone but herself.
Her scars which never healed,
slowly and quietly faded away.
Emotions overflowing
as the pain she carries became too heavy.

9. Always and Never

Always a choice, never the chosen
Always the listener, never heard
Always the lover, never the loved
Always trying, never enough
Always the one capturing moments,
while I wish someone would do that for me.
Not when I ask, not when I pose, just randomly.
Someone who likes to record me,
someone who notices the little things I do.
Like how I dance to the music in the shop,
how I laugh a bit too loud,
how I smile at the moon and
my little dance when I eat something delicious.

10. Endless Love

Just a romantic soul, waiting for something,
Hugging and holding hands.
Watching movies together and sharing drinks,
Deep talks and sharing smiles.
Laying your head on their shoulders,
and giving heartfelt handwritten notes.
Dancing like there's no tomorrow.
Sharing food,cooking together,
and finding the taste of your soul
These are the things my heart yearns for.

11. Behind the glow

The moon is so beautiful, it takes your eyes to another world
but nobody really seems to see the efforts of the sun.
The one who burns for the moon to shine.
Just like everyone who pass by the hardships I went through and just appreciates my succes, not my efforts.
The moon holds no blame but the sun's sacrifice often gets forgotten, just like everyone forgets the ones who sacrificed for them.
And that's why the sun should be appreciated as much as the moon so it never burnts out.

12. Just somebody

I just flow through life,
without living it.
I'm someone whose popular,
but nobody really knows.
I'm someone who just wants to be noticed,
loved and to be heard.
I hide in my own shadows,
waiting for my time to shine.
As soon as I say I'm alone,
everyone comes around pretending to be something they
are not.
I want love but I hesitate,
I don't wanna cry but my tears pours down.

13. Moments like smoke

Everything is temporary in this world,
time, money, happiness, success and
We don't know when our clock stops nor when someone
leaves you.
So stop expecting, stop oversharing,
stop and take a deep breath.
take everything in slowly
one by one
As time flows, everyone changes,
accept it,
it is what it is..
You can't change the rules of life
and life won't wait for us,
as time fades away like smoke.

14. Love, a gift from god

Something that's inside everyone,
where some hide it
and some kept it open.
Oh! to be loved by someone...
It's a divine feeling knowing,
that there is someone you love waiting for you.
Love, it's a gift that every human possess,
a gift from god.
The kind of love which makes you warm,
The kind of love which makes you blush,
The kind of love which makes you laugh,
The kind of love which makes you
love life a bit more than yesterday.
That kind of love is something we all search for...

15. Whispers of the Eldest Daughter

The one who grew up too fast,
A bit too mature,
Responsible and understanding.
The easy child,
whose childhood slipped away too fast,
the people pleaser.
First to smile and first to cry,
bearing the weight with a quite smile,
leading the way through storms.

16. Threads of Joy

While everyone passes by,
I find joy in the smallest things.
The smell of earth after rain,
the laughter that echoes between friends,
the silence in every eye contact,
the warm sun,
the stars shining bright,
a strangers fleeting smile,
the joy when you read your old diary,
the comfort of home,
the feeling of calmness when it's raining,
and mom's endless love.
These are some of my little joys...

17. Dear Lord

Dear lord..
When i get to heaven,
please let me be there with you.
Let me walk holding your hand and never let go,
let me follow your path and never get lost,
let the angels guide me so I never fall,
let me be one of your child,
So that I can be with you at peace.

18. Raindrops

Raindrops fall down my cheeks,
reminding me of my tears.
The tiny drops which have different meanings,
Tears of love,
Tears of happiness,
Tears of sadness,
Tears of anger,
Tears of helplessness and many more
And then there is the raindrops,
falling down like never tomorrow.
Raindrops like tears of earth,
refreshing and cooling down our earth,
Sacrificing onself for others,
Just like a mother.

19. Regret's silent song

I wish i did that,
I wish i didn't,
I wish i said that,
I wish i didn't,
I wish, I wish, I wish
This feeling of regret that won't go away,
it's a quiet, unending guest,
that sits in my chest and never rests.
Do it or don't,
say it or not.
Turn past mistakes into new open doors.

20. Bloom anyway

Treat yourself like a flower,
When it's hard to heal, drink water
Step into the gentle warmth of the sunshine,
visit bees and butterflies.
Surround yourself with other warm flowers.
You don't need to compete with other flowers,
as a garden has flowers of all sizes, colours and flowers
that bloom in different seasons.
It doesn't matter when,
but its never too late to bloom.
Rainy days may be tiring,
but they help you grow.
Just like a flower,
people care for you and find comfort in you.
So bloom with confidence,
even if you are in doubt,
bloom anyway.

21. A palette of emotions

Feelings like a roller coaster
going up and down.
sadness like a quite ache,
anger roaring inside,
happiness like a flower blooming,
confusion like being lost in the ocean
awkwardness like a smile too late
and words too slow,
Fear tiptoeing through the chest,
guilt a shadow that follows.
A human with many emotions,
like a rainbow with many colours

www.ingramcontent.com/pod-product-compliance
Lightning Source LLC
Chambersburg PA
CBHW051002030426
42339CB00007B/451